Daughters of Dawn by Bliss Carman

Co-Authored by Mary Perry King

"What cannot he said can he sung,
What cannot he sung can he danced"

William Bliss Carman was born in Fredericton, in New Brunswick on April 15th 1861. He was educated at Fredericton Collegiate School before moving to the University of New Brunswick, obtaining his B.A. there in 1881. As is common with so many writers his first published piece was for the University magazine and for Carman that was in 1879.

After several years editing various magazines and periodicals Carman first published a poetry volume in 1893 with Low Tide on Grand Pré. There was no Canadian company prepared to publish and when an American company did so it went bankrupt.

The following year was decidedly better. His partnership with the American poet Richard Hovey had given birth to Songs of Vagabondia. It was an immediate success.

That success prompted the Boston firm, Stone & Kimball, to reissue Low Tide on Grand Pré and to hire Carman as the editor of its literary journal, The Chapbook.

Carman brought out, in 1895, Behind the Arras, a somewhat more serious and philosophical work centered on the premise of a long meditation, using the speaker's house and its many rooms, as a symbol of life and the choices to be made.

In 1896 Carman met Mrs Mary Perry King, who rapidly became patron, adviser and sometime lover. She also became his writing collaborator on two verse dramas.

In 1897 Carman published Ballad of Lost Haven, and in 1898, By the Aurelian Wall, the title poem itself was an elegy to John Keats and the book was a collection of formal elegies.

As the century turned Carman was hard at work on a five-volume set of poetry "Pans Pipes". The excellence of a number of these poems did much to install Carman as the most noted of Canadian Poets and eventually their own Poet Laureate.

In 1912 the final work in the Vagabondia series was published. Richard Hovey had died in 1900 and so this last work was purely Carman's. It has a distinct elegiac tone as if remembering the past works themselves.

On October 28th, 1921 Carman was honored by the newly-formed Canadian Authors' Association where he was crowned Canada's Poet Laureate with a wreath of maple leaves.

William Bliss Carman died of a brain hemorrhage at the age of 68 in New Canaan on the 8th June, 1929.

Index of Contents

DEDICATION

TO HENRIETTA HOVEY WITH HOMAGE AND AFFECTION IN HAPPY APPRECIATION OF HER SERVICE TO THE CAUSE OF ART

INTRODUCTION

In rereading one of Edward Carpenter's wise books the other day I came upon the following suggestive passages, which express very well the thought underlying the Daughters of Dawn:

"Far back out of the brows of Greek goddess, and Sibyl, and Norse and German seeress and prophetess, over all this petty civilization look the grand untamed eyes of a primal woman the equal and the mate of man; and in sad plight should we be If we might not already, lighting up the horizon from East and West and South and North, discern the answering looks of those newcomers who, as the period of women's enslavement Is passing away, send glances of recognition across the ages to their elder sisters."

"The Greek goddesses look down and across the ages to the very outposts beyond civilization; and already from America, Australasia, Africa, Norway, Russia, as even in our midst from those who have crossed the border-line of all class and caste, glance forth the features of a grander type — fearless and untamed — the primal merging into the future Woman; who will help us to undo the bonds of death which encircle the present society, and open the doors to a new and a wider life."

Daughters of Dawn, literally written in collaboration, was originally planned by Mrs. King to serve as a series of studies in her new educational movement, in which the three rhythmic arts, poetry, music, and dancing, or interpretive motion, are combined for artistic and cultural purposes. Even if I had originated such a work and been rash enough to begin it alone, I could not unaided have given it anything like its present effectiveness, veracity, and conciseness, nor many of the beauties of thought and expression which I am glad to think it possesses. As there appeared to be no more appropriate name for dances or small motion dramas of this sort, in which the interpretation of the spoken verse is furthered simultaneously by adapted music and rhythmic motion which may or may not include dancing, we have been calling them Rhythmics.

Of the great company of illustrious women of the ages, many others might also have been chosen for such a work. These Daughters of Dawn were selected as typical chiefly of the liberal and beneficent power of woman's nature in her leadership and ascendancy in the life of the spirit and the destiny of the world. Selection was made of episodes lyrical rather than dramatic in feeling and significance, as most readily lending themselves to lyric treatment in verse, music, and motion.

Our best thanks are due to friends for generous aid in creating the various roles — to Miss Irmgard von Rottenthal for her poetic study of Eve, to Miss Hedwig Reicher for her masterly studies of Deborah and Balkis, to Miss Mirzah Chesllr for her studies of Sappho and a truly wonderful Mary, to Miss Ray Cohen for her exquisite interpretation of Izeyl, to Mrs. Bayard Redfield for her fine conception of Zenobia, to Miss Dorothy Dean for her most adequate Jeanne d'Arc, and to Miss Gertrude Lynch for her very gracious rendering of Vittoria Colonna. Our grateful acknowledgments belong also to Mr. B. J. Falk, who brought the interest of an old friend and the painstaking skill of an artist to the making of the photographic studies from which the illustrations are taken.

The writing of the various scenes, prologues, and choruses, and the selection and arrangement of the costumes, involved painstaking to insure their historic accuracy and consistency, so far as might be. In the different meters used in the dialogues an attempt has been made to secure in each case a verse form expressionally appropriate to the scene. These are but working considerations, but they may prove of service to students who may wish to use the Pageant at any time.

Bliss Carman
New Canaan, Connecticut,
October, 1912.

DAUGHTERS OF DAWN

OPENING PROLOGUE AND CHORUS

PERSONS IN THE PROLOGUE AND CHORUSES
TIME
A POET

[As the curtain rises on a front scene **TIME** and **A POET** enter from the left. **TIME** walks a little in advance of his companion and moving toward the centre of the stage delivers the prologue.

OPENING PROLOGUE
In the crystal sphere of time that swings through space

All loveliness survives. Each ardent grace,
Joyance, and noble passion, leaves its trace
Imperishable there.

And he who gazes In that magic glass
May see the pageant of the ages pass,
Vivid and glad and glorious as It was,
In its great hours of flare.

In scarlet tatters and in webs of gold.
Heroic ecstasies and dramas old,
Their core of wisdom and high glamour hold,
To bid men choose and dare.

[With the conclusion of his speech, **TIME** passes on across the stage to exit at the right. Music at once takes up the theme of the prologue and leads into the theme of the lyric chorus. As it ceases, the chorus follows, spoken by the **POET**, who does not move far from his place of entrance.

OPENING CHORUS
Who are these who pass by
With victorious mien,
Deathless light in the eye,
Fadeless glory and sheen
In their mystical beauty and bearing; their power to bless or to ban?

These are they who aspired
And were wise in their day,
Daring all they desired
Through din and dismay.
To foster the hope and the vision, — their share in the infinite plan.

They dreamed and endured
To bring gladness to birth.
That joy might be lured
From the sorrow of earth,
For the making of ever new Edens, to perfect what creation began.

They cherished the spark;
They protected the flame
From the winds and the dark;
To them the word came;
Their bodies were altars of love, and their faith was the rapture of man.

Whether beauty and truth
Were the stars of their power.
Or the ardor of youth.
Or the pride of the hour,
They broldered the banners they followed, while the sands of the hour-glass ran.

So from age unto age
Their beauty shall glow,
To brighten the page
Of earth's warfare and woe,
As the stars In the arches of heaven illumine the darkness they span.

[At the conclusion of this chorus the **POET** retires, and music follows with a glorification of the general theme of the Pageant.

[The same procedure is followed at the beginning of the various scenes. **TIME** speaking the prologues, and the **POET** reciting the lyric choruses, — with only this difference, that at the close of each chorus the curtain rises immediately, disclosing a realization of the **POET'S** vision, while the speaker makes his exit with eyes on the scene or remains half-concealed near his place of entrance, as an onlooker.

I.

EVE

PERSONS IN THE SCENE
EVE
ADAM

EVE

PROLOGUE
Lone in the strangeness of a dim new world,
Untutored, unbefrlended, alien, man
Moved to his destiny of perilous power
Between his ecstasies of hope and fear.
And wonder was upon him, and desire.

His strength was spent on rock and tree in vain;
His running reached no goal but loneliness;
Silent derision waited on his toll;
And ever the world-sorrow bore him down,
His great heart beaten by futility.

Then on a morning after monstrous storm,
A spirit whispered through the great dumb blue,
And there emerged among the gentle hills,
Loving, humane, mysterious, the form
Of beauty made in likeness of his dream.

Music

CHORUS
Who IS this ardor-paled
O'er her blood's coral stain,
Veiled as mountains are veiled
In a mist of blue rain?
She is fair as the great winter moonlight, and frail as Aprlllan flowers.

In her eyes there are gleams
Of the sun and the sea.
And unfathomed dreams
Of the ages to be;
Her beauty and wind-shod exulting take little account of the hours.

She moves like the drifts
Of fog on the tide.
Or the faint smoke that lifts
From the purple hillside;
And men at her beauty shall wonder, while wonder and beauty abide.

She fears not the portal
Of life nor of death;
She is tender and mortal
And subtle as breath;
And her voice Is the call of the ages that quickens this substance of ours.

Her love is a thing
Without hate or regret,
Yet In twilights of spring
Will her eyelids be wet
With strange immemorial sorrow. She is Eve of the mystical powers.

[A wooded glade in Paradise. A running stream through a meadow. The sea line in the distance. Birds, butterflies, flowers, and creatures. Morning sunlight. **EVE** appears among the trees, and accompanies her soliloquy with primitive expressive motion. At its close **ADAM** is seen through the trees, and speaks.

EVE
Dear life! Earth and sun and sea-line!
Shadowy woods and shining river!
Flowers and meadows fresh with morning,
Calling birds that sway and flutter,
Soaring glad and free!

What Is all this wonder round me,
With Its ravishing enchantment?
The leaves whisper; the grey water

Murmurs to the blue day; all things
Promise more and more.

And this mist of gold about me?
Running and seeing her reflection in the stream
I am swift . . . and light . . . and comely.
Like the birds, I call. Come, wander
Like the creatures! What am I, and
What are these to me?

Lovely sun, shine warm upon me!
Unseen wind, come and caress me!
Good earth, kiss my feet and take me
On long journeys, day and night-time,
Gladly everywhere.

Nothing answers to my calling!
Nothing solaces my longing!
Why are all things unresponding?
Why Is all my being lonely?
Is this Paradise?

Through the shadows there's a shadow
Coming. Through the trees I see him . . .
Like me . . . stronger! Ah, his presence
Makes me gladder, gladder, gladder . . .
What am I to thee?

ADAM

Have I not imaged thy face
Out of the sunrise and dreams?
Have I not sought thy trace.
Through the spring woods and streams?
The print in the vanishing dew,
The call that died on the air,
Lured me ever anew,
But never thyself was there.

I stretched forth hands to the sun,
I breathed my prayer through the rain,
I called to the clouds that run;
They answered me not again.
I have heard at the world's far edge
The great winds boom and moan;
I have harked to the whispering sedge;
But they spoke in a tongue unknown.

And ever the throbbing ache

Beat in my throat and side: —
The hunger I could not slake,
The craving that would not bide;
And ever the gleaming choice
Drew me forth on the trail,
Where never a kindred voice
Answered my desolate hail.

Thy glistening bosom swells
In the light of thy wondrous hair,
Like a sunlit hilltop that tells
The watcher day is there.
The croon of thy voice like the wind,
The sway of thy body like fire.
The glory of man shall bind
To the soul of thy desire.

Here let the sun stand still,
The wandering stream be stayed,
The shadow rest on the hill,
The wind play low in the glade!
For I have found Paradise,
And dread has lost its power.
Here let the great moon rise
On an enchanted hour!

Curtain and Music

II.

DEBORAH

Twelfth Century B. C.

PERSONS IN THE SCENE
DEBORAH
BARAK
CAPTAINS and Chief MEN of Israel

DEBORAH

PROLOGUE
The ages pass, and with enormous wars,
Sorrows and triumphs and enduring toll,

The earth-child Man puts off his savagery,
And with the growing wisdom of the earth
Learns law and artistry and paths to power.

He builds In Egypt mammoth pyramids;
In Babylon his gilded temples rise;
Till strength and beauty fill his heart with pride.
Then comes a nomad people with their tents,
Dreamers and wanderers with flocks and herds.

Captive, oppressed, arrogant and unsubdued,
Forever cherishing their racial dream.
Out of the desert, seeking pasturage.
To the rich valleys of the West they come, —
The tribes of Israel to their promised land.

Music

CHORUS
What prophetess stands,
With God's fire in her eyes
And His love in her hands,
As she signals and cries
The word that shall summon her people to turn back a tyrannous might?

In beauty austere,
With her hood half withdrawn.
She is straight as a spear.
Or a shaft of the dawn.
When it flushes the cedars of Kedron, and floods the dark valleys with light.

Her voice has the spell
Of the wind and the rain.
She sways with the swell
Of the ripe-breasted grain.
When summer is red in the valleys and his fervors are fierce on the plain.

To the South and the North,
Fleet runners light-shod
At her bidding went forth
With the war-cry of God
That should kindle the hearts of the tribes as a watch-fire kindles the night.

Let princes give heed
And their kingdoms make way,
When a woman at need
Goes down to the fray!
For Deborah, rousing a nation, the God of her fathers will fight.

[Outside the tent of Deborah in Mount Ephraim between Ramah and Bethel. A running brook is near by. ther tents and distant hills are seen. **DEBORAH** stands under a palm tree in front of her door; before her, **CHIEF MEN** of Israel, including **BARAK** the son of Abinoam from Kedesh-Naphtali in the North,

DEBORAH
O captains and chiefs of Zebulon,
And rulers of Naphtall, hear!
And Barak son of Abinoam,
Thou warrior-leader, draw near!

What the Lord God of Israel speaketh
By the palm tree In Ramah this day,
By the mouth of Deborah His servant,
Ye shall hearken unto and obey.

For the voice of the Lord in the morning,
Before the first sun took the dew
From the valleys and ridges of Hermon, —
While the peaks of the East were still blue, —
Came to me, as I stood in the tent-door
Thinking on Israel's wrong.
And God said, "I have seen the oppression.
But behold, it shall not be for long.

"Send thou to Kedesh for Barak,
And bid him unsheath the sword
Against the outrage of Jabln.
And I will prosper my word."
Who halted the sun over Gibeon,
The moon above Ajalon's plain?
Who strengthened the ox-goad of Shamgar,
By whom the six hundred were slain?

So shall ye prevail against evil.
Their chariots of Iron shall flee.
The floods shall break them in pieces
And roll them into the sea.
The vineyards and fields of these Gentiles
Shall be added unto your lands,
For the stars in their courses shall aid you
And deliver them into your hands.

Go, get you up to the mountains,
Let ten thousand follow your feet.
And I will make ready the captive,
For the day Is at hand. Be fleet.

There is a star in the crowd,
O Barak, who makest the torches
In the temple at Shiloh to shine,
Wilt thou not carry the fire
To free thy people and mine?

Have I stood here for judgment and council
And prophesied truly, in vain?
Are my words but as wind of the desert,
My talk but as running of rain?
Is there none to accomplish my vision?
Is there none to believe what I see?
Am I a babbler of Baal?
O Barak, what am I to thee?

BARAK
O Deborah, for judgment
The tribes come up to thee,
The tents all know thy wisdom
From Jordan to the sea.
In the hills thy name is spoken,
By the rivers it Is heard.
The captains seek thy counsel,
The wayward heed thy word.

And when I set the torches
To light the Holy Place,
They pale as I remember
The glory of thy face.
But three days since at sunrise
Did thy messenger draw nigh
Breathless before the doorway,
To seek me. Here am I.

In the light of this thy counsel,
What shall thy servant do.
But carry the dread summons
To raise the tribes anew?
As thy soul lives, among them
The word of God shall pass,
As fire among the stubble.
As wind among the grass,

Only if thou go with me!
Else here I will abide.
I have nor hope nor portion
That Is not by thy side.
Mine Is the strength to conquer,

And mine the skill of hand.
But not the inward knowledge
To see and understand.

Then take thy staff and mantle.
Make fast thy sandal-thong,
For thou shalt teach me wisdom.
And I will make thee strong.
Deborah makes a sign of assent.
O peerless among women.
There is no other way
Since God In the beginning
Breathed spirit into clay.

[Here a religious dance begins. The multitude grows, and forms behind **DEBORAH** and **BARAK** for final exit.

So go we up before Him
To the hills, ten thousand strong
And I will lead the fighting,
And thou shalt lift the song.
The ages shall remember,
When we are plunged in night,
How Deborah and Barak
Did battle for the Light.

Curtain and Music

III.

BALKIS

Tenth Century B. C.

PERSONS IN THE SCENE
BALKIS, Queen of Sheba
SOLOMON, King of Israel
Musicians and Attendants

BALKIS

PROLOGUE
Egypt, Assyria, Chaldaea pass
Across the world's great stage from dark to dark.

With sound of drum and flash of marching spears,
Amid the stumbling outcries of the poor.
And all the splendid pomp of barbarous kings;

While Israel, cleaving to her lofty faith
In one pure God of justice and of right.
Is scorned and driven on, beaten and bruised
Under the harrow of the conqueror's hate;
Through centuries of carnage, lust, and gloom.

Till from that turmoil, as from evil dreams,
In Judah rose a king, humanely wise
Above all men. And Rulers of the Dusk,
In their far countries hearing of the Light,
Up to Jerusalem in wonder came.

Music

CHORUS
In crimson and gold
By the ivory throne,
Who IS she who makes bold,
With a pride all her own,
To prove with hard questions the wisdom that
fame has made first in the land?

As the twelve lions gaze
And the thurifers swing.
She stands in amaze
Before the great king.
And her strength is as water, beholding his
splendor and knowledge expand.

Her walk has the sway
Of a sea in the wind, —
The strong supple play
Of a panther of Ind, —
The magic of might is about her; her sorcery
who shall withstand!

By the long camel trains
Bearing gifts above price.
All the wealth of the plains,
Silver, algum and spice.
And purple and gold without measure, and
peacocks, and pearls by the strand, —

By her garments all bright.

By her gems from Kanaugh,
Her luxurious height.
And her swarthy low brow.
It IS Balkis, dark Queen of Sheba. By the
ring it is Solomon's hand.

[Wooded grounds outside of Solomon's palace. The Queen of Sheba's **MUSICIANS** and **ATTENDANTS**
enter playing, walking backward. As **BALKIS** enters from the palace, after her meeting with Solomon, she
beckons them impatiently to precede her. They go off quickly, leaving her alone.

BALKIS
King, I, Balkis, Queen of Sheba, came to greet thee from afar, —
Feel thy sway and know thy wisdom and thy splendor as they are.
All the unmatched wealth and glory of thy House I would behold;
And I brought thee royal treasure, gems and frankincense and gold.
But an overpowering grandeur and a strange unearthly lore
That surround thee, have undone me with a spell unknown before.
Whence are they? And how should any mortal being so outshine
Pomp and pride and power of armies — all earth's riches — his or mine?
Where Is all my strong assurance which the desert knew in fear?
What befell my proven knowledge keen as a dividing spear?
Am I a fond girl before him, hand to tremble, cheek to pale.
That his speech should shake my heartstrings like a palm grove in a gale?
Great Earth, give me back my courage I Desert wind and sun, renew
The wild strength of heart that made me as unquestioning as you I
Has that sorcery departed, with Its soft relentless skill,
That could sway the blood of princes till they bowed before my will?
No more I For my tyranny Is vanquished. All I was, is naught.
Like the play of pampered children seem the ends for which I wrought.
All my trappings and my triumphs are as faggots without flame.
Like a road from night to morning seems the way by which I came.
Life beyond me, take my homage, as the sun drinks from the stream!
Light of God beyond my learning, teach one who has caught thy gleam!
As the day consumes the desert, as the strong wind bends the tree.
Lord of Light, thou hast enslaved me! Great King I What am I to thee?

[**BALKIS** goes out slowly following after her train of **ATTENDANTS** and **RETAINERS**. As she disappears,
palace music is heard and Solomon's **MUSICIANS** enter playing, walking backward.

[The **KING** enters speaking, and dismisses his **ATTENDANTS** with a gesture,

SOLOMON
Balkis, Queen of thy kind, I must find thee again.
I have sought in the sound of the flute and the harpstring in vain
The enchantment that lurks in thy voice for the stirring of man!
No fire of gems like thine eyes, no dye like thy tan!
What gives thee thy lustre, like amber aglow with old wine?
What perfume of cedar, of sunshine and summer is thine?

The palpitant sense of thy presence is still on the air.
My fir-trees have caught the blue shadows that lurk in thy hair.
Who taught thee that sibylline quiet which teases my power.
As the strength of soft winds the ocean uplifts in an hour?
Thy leonine courage, thy query that throbs to the mark,
Are fires of new revelation, enkindling the dark.
Thy gifts hold the glamour of giving that dwells in thy hand;
Thy tribute no kingship could merit; stay thou in our land!
My realm Is a desert without thee to set it abloom;
My skill is but dull, since It caught not thy wit in Its loom.
Come, give me thine ardor that leaps from the lip to the heart!
Come, teach me the tremor of eyelids where tears wait to start!
Come, tell me the word that was spoken when Lucifer fell!
There is naught at the source of dominion thou knowest not well.

[At the end of his soliloquy **SOLOMON** goes out, following the direction taken by Balkis.

Curtain and Music

IV.

SAPPHO

Sixth Century B. C.

PERSONS IN THE SCENE
SAPPHO
PHAON
ATTHIS   }
ANACTORIA   }
GYRINNA   }
GORGO   }
DICA   }
TELESIPPA   } Friends of Sappho
MNASIDICA   }
MYRTO   }
LAIS   }
MYRTOCLEIA }
BACCHIS   }
CHRYSIS   ]

SAPPHO

PROLOGUE

While Israel cringed to dread Omnipotence,
And dwelt in fear of the unspoken name;
While priests of Egypt pondered on the past,
And Nineveh was sinking to her doom;
The day was spreading on the Ægean sea,

Where white-sailed Tyrlan coasters plied with trade,
And glad young Hellas hailed the wakening light.
There beyond marble cliffs where jonquils grew.
Were rosy porticos and temples dim
With mellow Ivory and dusky gold.

Her gardens odorous with hyacinth.
Her river-beds ablaze with pomegranate.
Her groves of laurel spreading In the sun,—?
There like a tulip where the flame of life
Burns quick and clear, bloomed Lesbos of the Isles.

Music

CHORUS

Who is this with life-thirst
In her luminous eyes, —
Whose rapture unnursed
Burns quickly and dies,
As the dew burned away from the morning leaves only the color and fire?

She is vibrant and warm
As a meadow at noon;
She Is lonely as storm,
Or the cloud-sailing moon;
She is glad as new friendship unbroken, and sad as old loves that expire.

She Is swift as a thrush,
The noiseless of wing,
When the damp woodlands gush
With his lyric of spring.
She dances like small meadow rivers that run through the twilight and sing.

This is Sappho. Men gave
To new-minted gold
Her image to save
For the peoples untold,
That her beauty might ever companion the echoing chords of her lyre.

Though all lovely things
To the dust shall be traced,

And the names of great kings
From their tombs be effaced.
Her name shall be fresh through the ages as Spring rains on the ruins of Tyre.

[The garden of Sappho's house in Lesbos, with marble benches, a green space, borders of daffodils, hyacinths, violets and other spring flowers. The sea and the harbor of Mytilene in the distance. A wall at the foot of the garden, with a gate into the street. The house is of white marble, with a low doorstep on a level with the ground. It is afternoon.

[Enter from another part of the garden **ATTHIS, ANACTORIA, GYRINNA, GORGO, DICA, TELESIPPA, MNASIDICA, MYRTO, LAIS, MYRTOCLEIA, BACCHIS,** and **CHRYSIS**, friends of Sappho.

ANACTORIA
How warm the new sun is!

CHRYSIS
Surely it is full time
To honor our Adonis!

DICA
Where is Sappho?

ATTHIS
Sappho!

[They **ALL** call in unison.

Sappho! Sappho! Sappho!

[Enter **SAPPHO** from the house.

SAPPHO
Sweet friends! Has the sunshine
Lit thoughts of Adonis
In your lovely heads?

Bring thy lute, Gyrinna!
Dica, bring thy garlands!
And thy golden jonquils,

Chrysis!l Myrtoclela,
Dance here at my left hand!
Thou here, dearest Atthis!
Myrto shall be chorus,
With her silver voice.

Anactorla, thou
Ardentest of lovers —

[**ANACTORIA** embraces her.

Thy sweet call would waken
The sleepiest Adonis!
Oh, these happy hours
Of the spring In Lesbos!
Surely he must harken
To our chorus now.

[They dance, joining in the refrain of **MYRTO'S** Hymn to Adonis.

Now the winter Is gone by.
And the swallow builds again,
(Lovely Adonis!)
Now the quickening sun is warm,
And the wind Is soft with rain.
(Lovely Adonis!)
Now the waking earth is sweet
With the scent of purple flowers.
(Thou sweet Adonis!)
All the buds are opening wide,
Wasting through the golden hours.
(Thou fond Adonis!)
Now the nightingales are come,
With their piercing flutes of gold;
(Beloved Adonis!)
And thy lovers cry to thee,
In their passion, as of old.
(Cruel Adonis!)
Call him back across the years I
He is fairer than the day.
(Hear us, Adonis!)
Love, ah, love, — Is anything
Half so sweet, for all men say?
(Harken, Adonis!)
Fling his robe of frost aside.
And his bands of sleep unbind I
(Waken, Adonis!)
Were they lovelier long ago,
Those who loved thee — or more kind?
(Love us, Adonis I)
Cherish him with tender fire
In the woodlands of the spring,
(Deathless Adonis I)
And with him assuage desire.
Ah, Is love so fleet a thing?
(Lovely Adonis I)

[Street music is heard.

CHRYSIS
Hark, a tambourine!

ATTHIS
The street musicians!

ANACTORIA
That's the boy from NaxosI O the darling!
Do you love him, DIca, — or the dark one
With the captive woodbird? He Is thine.

CHRYSIS
They are moving on now.

ANACTORIA
Let us follow!

[They run off, laughing. When they are gone, **SAPPHO** sits on a bench, beginning to be sad. The
afternoon is waning.

SAPPHO
Ah, me! . . . May Adonis
Find them! . . . This soft spring wind
Makes my fillet heavy.

[She loosens her hair.

Thou dear swallow flashing
Over Mytilene,
Art thou never weary
All the blinding day long
In our Northern blue?

She sings

If death be good,
Why do the gods not die?
If life be ill,
Why do the gods still live?
If love be naught,
Why do the gods still love?
If love be all,
What should men do but love?

What a thing Is woman

In this world! All music,
Ecstasy, and dreaming.
With her gems and garlands.
Gauze and gold! All dancing,
And bright laughter, bubbling
Like a silver fountain
Out of the dark earth!

And her friendships, — stories
Told to amuse children!
Shadows that fly seaward!
All the while her heart aches
Only with one longing.
One demand . . . O Phaon,
Thou art so long absent
From this empty world!

In just such lovely weather
He would come with evening.
To sit here all happy . . .
I could hear him far off
In the fragrant twilight,

[A flute is heard in the distance'

Ere he crossed the meadow.
The playing grows more distinct.
O, praise Aphrodite!
Phaon!

[Enter **PHAON**.

Phaon! Phaon!
What am I to thee?

PHAON
O my Sappho I Heart of gladness,
What should thy soul do with sorrow?
See, I bring thee gems from Egypt,
Phrygian linen white as sea-foam,

Scarlet cloth from Tyre;
Eastern perfumes, and a girdle
Of wrought gold from ancient Sidon.
Not a port but has paid tribute
To thy beauty, in the sea-bales

[They unlade for thee.

SAPPHO

Only one gift have the high gods given
To man, Phaon, without stint or question,
As my heart knows, — love.
Thou art all my Egypt and my Sidon.
Earth and sea have paid me their full tribute,
If thou love me still.

PHAON

Sappho, not an isle from Rhodes to Imbros,
Not a pine-dark headland where the foam breaks,
But has heard the prayers and eager vows I whispered
Day and night for thee.

When I walked through splendid sunlit cities,
My lone heart was traversing a desert,
And the murmuring throngs were but as moving sand-drifts,
Sappho, without thee.

Nevermore, till the dread hour shall part us,
May I be beyond thy call, thy hand-touch I
Thou art all about me like the sweet dusk wheeling
Up from the great sea.

[They go into the house. Night is falling.

Curtain and Music

V.

IZEYL

Fifth Century B. C.

PERSONS IN THE SCENE
IZEYL
BUDDHA
A MAN-SERVANT of Izeyl
Two DISCIPLES of Buddha.
ATENDANTS and House SERVANTS of Izeyl

IZEYL

PROLOGUE

The Himalayas, Dwellings of the Snow,
Look down on all the fertile Ganges plain,
Where, spreading like a flood from high Pamir
Seeking new land, the Aryan drift went by,
Singing glad Vedas while the world was young.

Then rose the priestly Brahman over them
With bonds of caste, stern ritual and rule,
The sterile rites and dull formalities.
That would enslave the incarnate soul of man
And blight the progress of a growing world.

Here, having pity for the plight of men
And all their futile agonies of life.
Came Buddha, the Enlightened in the Way,
Preaching Renunciation of Desire,
The only surety of an earthly peace.

Music

CHORUS

Who stands In the dusk
Of the courtesan's square,
With an odor of musk
In her bosom and hair,
With anklets of turquoise and silver that clink for the passer to hear?

Mysterious as night,
With her hot scarlet mouth,
And a glittering light
In those eyes of the South,
As if all of her exquisite being had never one hunger to fear!

She moves like the smoke.
As it swoons on still air.
When the censers evoke
Old gods from their lair;
The sway of her body is music more maddening than incense or prayer.

The desire of the heart.
The delight of the eye,
She knows not apart,
To forego nor deny,
For love Is the sum of her being, and beauty is all of her gear.

Ah, fear her not I Hers
Is that passion of soul

Which no height deters,
No terrors control, —
Izeyl, the enamored of Buddha, who waits for her god to draw near.

[The courtyard in front of Izeyl's house in the Deer Forest north of Benares. A large rug is spread is the centre of the court, a low divan at one side, with small tables or benches near it. On the opposite side, a wall and gateway, the main entrance to the grounds. It is moonlight. **SERVANTS** enter carrying silver dishes of rice, fruits, and confections, basins and jugs of water, towels, etc, and set them down on the tables and the ground. **IZEYL** with two **ATTENDANTS** enters from the house.

IZEYL
Make all ready. Let there be nothing lacking nor amiss.
Though we have had many guests, there was never one like this.

[A man **SERVANT** enters from the gate, followed by **BUDDHA** and two **DISCIPLES** who approach and bow to **IZEYL**.

Welcome, O enlightened one, to this house. A happy day
Brings thy footsteps to my door, bids thee tarry on thy way.
Lets me serve thee. That my lord's heart with gladness may be free,
Rest here in the perfumed dusk of the roses strewn for thee.

BUDDHA
Thy words are lavish as the wayside stars,
Shedding their bounty for the pilgrim night.
No goodlier seeds than kindness come to blossom
In this great world to be faint heart's delight.

[**SERVANTS** wait upon **BUDDHA**, remove his sandals, wash the dust from his feet, offer him food and drink. He takes a cup of water, but declines to eat. His **DISCIPLES** withdraw to a distant part of the court. The servants go out, except Izeyl's two personal **ATTENDANTS**, who stand hack by the house door.

IZEYL
Sit, Lord. I will dance for thee. Here until the moon grows pale
Thou shalt be the worshipped one, I thy worshipper Izeyl.

[She prepares to dance. The dance is one of the ancient dramatic dances of India, it portrays the first glimpse of the beloved, embarrassment, infatuation, coquetry, enticement, and the overtures of love. It then becomes more reckless in its sorceries, while the beloved still seems obdurate. The dance next betrays jealousy, anger, and finally melting sorrow and surrender.

Now the play Is Love. It moves like a wind among the trees,
Woman's drama of the soul, with mysterious melodies.
Fear as faltering as night, desire Imperious as day,
Hold Love at their mystic height, till wild joy must have Its way.
Love Is water for thy thirst, Love Is honey for thy mouth.
Is thy being never faint in a land of parching drouth?

Loose the girdle from her breast and the lotus from her hair!
Take her, for sweet life or death! Is there anyone more fair?

[She dances, and at the conclusion of her dance falls at **BUDDHA'S** feet.

Lo, my beauty at thy feet, and my hand upon thy knee,
In despair of love I lay. Buddha, what am I to thee?

[**BUDDHA** puts out his hand and touches her, as she remains seated near him on the ground.

BUDDHA
Thou art all beauty, glowing sense and spirit,
The world's supremest splendor and desire.
Thou art the flower-like joy, the flame-like passion
Whose breath consumes men with relentless fire.
Thou art the subtle unforgotten fragrance
That haunts this life with an assuaging power,
And would beguile the soul upon her journey.
To deify one perishable hour.

But I, compelled by sorrow for men's warfare
Against their bonds upon the wheel of life.
Through sore compassion found the Great Renouncement
The only strength to stay the ravenous strife.
Crave nothing! But in kindness with rejoicing
Follow the common highway unto peace.
There only can survive the flower of wisdom,
There only can serene love find release.

Whoso is tranquil, diligent, undaunted.
Not overcome with riches nor with cares.
Free from all anger, arrogance, and baseness.
Seeking the truth as one who climbs the stairs
Within a tower of outlook, while in all things
Serving his fellows with illumined mind, —
However slowly, shall escape from darkness.
And all the weight of sorrow leave behind.

For this I waited underneath the Bo-tree,
Keeping stern vigil through the holy night.
Until Truth dawned, as I beheld the snow-peaks
Flushed with a tender glory height on height.

[**BUDDHA** rises and paces to and fro, while **IZEYL** remains seated.

And yet the doubt comes — what avails the watching
Above the world in unimpassioned calm?
Do they not sometimes long, those soaring summits.

To wear the valley's wealth of bloom and balm?

Ah, not alone thy beauty moves my senses.
But the fair soul within thee calls my soul.
My manhood strains at touch of joy so tender
To lay aside the austere staff and bowl.

[The **SERVANT** of the gate enters and bows before **IZEYL**.

SERVANT
Protectress of the weak, the poor in throngs
Are crowding at the gate to lay their wrongs
Before the Holy One, their woes and wants.
Shall I give dole as unto mendicants?

IZEYL [rising]
Nay, I myself will give, who have this day
Received the wealth that passes not away.
Let them be fed. Take these, and these, and these, —

She pulls off her gold and jewelled ornaments and gives them to the **SERVANT**, her **WOMEN** at the same
time removing her anklets.

And all I have for their necessities.
Turn gold and gems to bread that men may live.
There still Is more, — I have my life to give.
Go, tell them that Izeyl became to-night
A follower of Buddha and the light.

[The **SERVANT** goes out and **IZEYL** turns to **BUDDHA**.

Now the undetermined way to perfection waits us still, —
Thou the sun upon the height, I the mist below the hill!
So, dear Lord, the play is done, as the moon begins to fail.
And thy worshipper departs. Thou shalt see no more Izeyl.
This, that was my house and park, for thy shelter is bestowed.
Love's provision for thy peace when a-weary of the road.

[She claps her hands, and her **ATTENDANTS** come forward, with the **SERVANT** of the gate, to wait upon
her departure,

BUDDHA
Thou wondrous prodigal, no merit worthy
Thy matchless bounty have I, who must pass.
Like a disturbing wind among the palm-leaves.
Like an unresting shadow from the grass.
But thy good deed, like a reviving perfume.

Within the memories of men shall dwell, —
Inspired abandon I May the Perfect Way
Requite thee I

IZEYL
O beloved one, farewell!

[She goes out, accompanied by her two **WOMEN**, who cover their faces with their saris in desolation, **BUDDHA** is left standing alone in the growing darkness.

Curtain and Music

VI.

MARY

PERSONS IN THE SCENE
MARY
The ANGEL At the Tomb

MARY

PROLOGUE
In the brief peace of the Augustan Age,
Three trends of human headway checked their course,
Like currents eddying in a tideless calm.
Eastern magnificence and mystic dream,
Hellenic learning and awakened art.

And Roman discipline, all came to halt.
As when unbridled revellers at dawn
Look wanly forth on time's expectant hush.
Stilled of a sudden in satiety.
The ancient world of lust and rapine seemed

To pale with prescience of impending doom.
Outside a Syrian rest-house, with no pomp
Save glittering troops of stars relieving guard,
A Prince of the Eternal Light was born,
Whose only ensign was a loving heart.

Music

CHORUS

What spirit so white,
With eyes bent on the ground,
As though lost in the plight
Of a sorrow profound,
That tenderness, faith, and devotion should
founder In death and dismay?

She lifts her worn face,
And the glory Is there, —
The mothering grace.
The victorious care.
That have fostered the hope of the ages and
prospered the world on its way.

Her fair mouth is still.
Her hands are at rest.
With that power to thrill.
By the quiet possessed.
When the soul to Its lord Is surrendered and
divinity swells in the breast.

O all who have prayed
To the glorious son
Of this poor Jewish maid,
Since her travail was done,
Have ye bred In your sons the high courage to
be heroes of truth in their day?

Have ye given brave thought
To bring beauty to birth?
Have ye suffered and wrought
For the welfare of earth?
So your service transfigured to glory, like
Mary's, shall not pass away.

[A rocky place before the sepulchre of Christ. The entrance to the tomb is on slightly rising ground at the back, with straight evergreen trees on either side. His mother is seated on a stone near by, clad in white, with a fold of her garment over her head. She scarcely moves until toward the close of her first speech. It is just before dawn on the morning of the 'third day' after the crucifixion.

MARY

Lord of the darkness and the broken heart,
In the still purple hour before the sun,
Upon whose floor our lives are sifted chaff,
And through whose hands the sands of ages run,
Thy will be done!

Shall there be no compassion in the night.
No heed nor hearing of our grievous doom,
No heart that feels the loneliness of ours.
No hope of tidings from the unknown tomb
To pierce the gloom?

After the anguish of defeat and death,
Through boundless desolation of the years.
Is there no sign to help us live or die,
No touch to wipe away the bitter tears.
And quiet fears?

Knows God the agony of mother pain
For every sorrow of the son she bore?
Can any cry to Heaven bring again
The voice they have entombed, and closed the door.
For evermore?

If mortal heart can bear the woe and wrong,
And still live on in sorrow day by day,
If broken lute can lift a duteous song,
Or darkened lamp still serve with dying ray,
Show thou the way!

Great God, thou seest the path I tread alone,
Thou knowest all that has been and shall be,
And all my love of Him who was thine own, —
What in thy mighty dream of destiny
Am I to thee?

[As she closes her speech, she rises and goes a step or two toward the tomb, lifting imploring arms aloft, the fold of her robe slipping from her head as she does so. She stands thus transfixed for a moment, facing the sepulchre, and then turns with a look of wonder, her arms still upstretched, her whole figure illumined in the first rays of the new sun, and her face transfigured with rapture of revelation. From the slightly higher ground she has taken, she looks taller, too, than her wont; so that passers-by might think they had seen an angel. She speaks in a level tone.

Mary [as The Angel]
Hail, Mary of Sorrows, acquainted with woe.
Lift thy grief-shadowed gaze to the light-bearing sun!
Each quivering leaf and the dawn winds that blow
Breathe solace upon thee; the victory's won;
Weep not!

Thy God holds thy hands as he holds night and day.
Through the rounds of his service, the ways to his ends;
When thine arms are weakest, his strength is thy stay.
Thine eyes shall see clear in the light that he sends.

Fear not!

Lift up thy soul on the wings of his voice,
Be glad thou wert chosen to play thy great part,
Bid all thy mothering patience rejoice.
Let the world rest on the strength of thy heart!
Faint not!

Conceived of divine love, the rapturous soul,
Stainless as dew and unfearing as fire,
From hope unto hope as the quickened years roll,
Shall arise and live on through dismay and desire.
Aspire!

The God of all good cannot waver nor sleep.
Receive the sweet truth that shall lighten thine eyes,
And be thou the Angel earth's courage to keep,
The great Loving-Kindness that lights Paradise!
Behold!

Shine on through the ages and arches of heaven.
For thine is a glorious share in God's plan!
Unto thee from the first to the last has been given
The illuming, the heartening, the moulding of man.
Rejoice!

[**MARY** keeps her prophetic pose until the curtain falls.

Curtain and Music

VII.

ZENOBIA

270 A. D.

PERSONS IN THE SCENE
ZENOBIA, Queen of Palmyra
AURELIAN, Emperor of Rome
A Troupe of Arab Dancing GIRLS and Musicians
Roman OFFICERS and SOLDIERS, LITTER-BEARERS, GUARDS, ATTENDANTS, etc.

ZENOBIA

PROLOGUE

Hark! To what sound like thunder far away
Do cities tremble and strong men turn pale?
They clutch the sword In Eastern palaces,
They lift the tent-fold on Arabian plains,
And start in forests of wild Gaul, to hear
The tramp of Roman legions through the world.
Then through the beauty of the star-sown night
An angry glare upon the sky proclaims
An opulent city given to the torch
Of ruthless conquerors on the march to power.

Where once men trafficked in the crowded streets,
And women chattered in the bright bazaars.
While children thronged the Temple of the Sun, —
The wild boar feeds among sad ruined walls
Of great Palmyra in the desert sands.

Music

CHORUS

Who is this come, in haste
From the crowds to be gone,
Through the Palmyrene waste,
While the legions draw on,
With tumult of murderous passions that conquering lust has released?

She sees at her gates
Roman standards unfurled,
Where once vassal states
Brought the trade of the world, —
Where long caravans o'er the desert came in from the marvellous East.

She stands like a palm
Aloof and unbent.
With the sky's royal calm
For her curtain and tent.
Her loveliness still undefeated, her regal devotion unspent.

Barbaric in splendor,
Heroic at heart.
Undaunted and tender,
She plays her great part,
Though the reins of her power are broken, the days of her empire have ceased.

Her beauty still reigns,
Though her hopes all have died.

Her fierce grandeur remains, —
The Bedouin pride, —
Zenobia, Queen of Palmyra, the coveted pearl of the East.

[In front of Aurelian's tent before Palmyra. The **EMPEROR** is seated, surrounded by a few
of his **GENERALS** and **OFFICERS**, A troupe of Arab dancing **GIRLS** and **MUSICIANS** run in to dance for
him. Before the close of their dance there is a stir outside and the hasty arrival of two **RUNNERS**
followed by a closed litter borne by eight **BEARERS**. They set down their burden and, assisted by
GUARDS, **ZENOBIA** alights with one **WOMAN** in waiting. At sight of her the dancing **GIRLS** at once stop
their dance and, ignoring the **EMPEROR**, run to **ZENOBIA**, kneel before her, and surround her with every
mark of loyal admiration, crying, 'Long life to Zenobia!' As **AURELIAN** rises and approaches **ZENOBIA**, a
trumpet sounds and **SERVANTS** and **DANCERS** withdraw.

AURELIAN
Fortunate is this hour, indeed! Happy the day for Rome,
When here unto Aurelian's tent the Queen of the East is come!

ZENOBIA
And dark for my country. Emperor!

AURELIAN
Nay, It had darker been.
Had not the gods delivered thee into my hands, brave Queen.

ZENOBIA
Aurelian, say not the gods preside over a thing so base
As the treachery which betrayed me here, a prisoner before thy face.
O, better far, had my luckless star gone down in the dust of fight, —
Had my glory passed unsoiled at last into eternal night!
And lordlier had thy legions shown above a broken wall,
Than skulking at a traitor's gate, let in at a scullion's call.
Since when did the Roman eagles deign to take a reptile's kill.
Like unclean vultures swooping low and greedy for their fill?
Had not black treason sold me here, like a Bithynian slave,
Palmyra should have been my tomb, her citadel my grave.
Zenobia would not have lived to be the spoil of war, —
To be the Forum's spectacle, in chains behind thy car.
Ye know the creed of the desert breed, whom none can bind nor bow.
Rovers of earth by right of birth, from the dawn of time till now.
But even the gods must strive in vain, at war with treachery.
Their altar fires are but the pyres of the daring and the free.

AURELIAN
You wrong the sons of the Roman wolf! They know the desert's way.
And well they know the proudest foe is a lioness at bay.
What evil councillors were thine to move thee to this war?
Did Rome not give you peace and wealth, — could liberty give more?
Have not your laden caravans brought all the world in trade

Up to your gates, with none to bar the roads that Trajan made?

ZENOBIA

Hear me, my captor! Had there been upon the Cassars' throne
One like Aurelian in days past, this discord had not grown.
While puny tyrants fought like knaves for the sceptre fallen low,
Was I to be their prize and fee? By the Immortals, No!
Bred to the freedom of the tents, born of a royal line,
I drew the tribes Into a Power. I made It. It was mine.
Here out of turbulence and strife a sovereign state I reared, —
Palmyra In the Wilderness, rich, beautiful, and feared.
Insolent Persia felt my will, even Imperial Rome
As empire unto empire in peace or war must come.
Could I lay by this sovereignty at a dictator's word?
Step lightly down from throne and crown, and join the driven herd?
Ceasing to reign, I cease to live. Does Aurelian wonder why?
Can a Caesar and a soldier ask? Need Zenobla reply?
Those poor dance girls with matted curls, that clung about my knee,
Shall grace my lord's triumphal march; but what am I to thee?

AURELIAN

Thy noble words, Zenobia, prove well thy royal strain.
I do lament the downfall of one so fit to reign.
Had not ambition duped thee, and thy guides who counselled ill,
Palmyra had been sovereign, and thou her ruler still.
Let not ambition lure you, my captains, to your fall.
Ever the overreaching hand must end by losing all.
Would that this restless folly which Is the whole world's bane
Might die with me, uprooted never to rise again!
Yet Is thy speech untempered, great leader of the tribes!
Unfair to Roman justice, thy bitter grief-wrung jibes.
Believe the lonely desert shall forget the morning star,
When Roman virtue has forgot what truth and honor are.
I were myself a traitor, had I not seized the hour
When renegade informers betrayed thee to our power.
Receive a soldier's tribute! Accept a Roman's word!

[A tumult is heard outside, A hand of unruly **SOLDIERS** clamoring for the life of **ZENOBIA**. A number of **OFFICERS** hurry out immediately and quell the disturbance.

Fear not my wayward legions. Thy guard shall be my sword.
No safer wert thou ever. Thou shalt go hence to Rome, —
There with respect and honor be welcome and at home.
And this thy noble city with its Temple of the Sun
Shall be preserved from pillage. For thy sake it is done.
Although thy rash advisers must pay their folly's cost;
Thou art no less an empress, for an empire's being lost.
The world awards thee homage!

ZENOBIA
Magnanimous, my foe!

AURELIAN
Thine Emperor attends thee. The lictors, there! We go.

[With her last word **ZENOBIA** turns away to enter her litter; but as she hears **AURELIAN** say 'Thine Emperor attends thee' she turns and looks into his face. Seeing that he is preparing to accompany her on foot, she signals her **BEARERS** to follow, and walks out by **AURELIAN'S** side, **BEARERS** and **ATTENDANTS** following.

Curtain and Music

VIII.

JEANNE d'ARC

1427 A. D.

PERSONS IN THE SCENE
JEANNE d'ARC
JACQUES d'ARC, Her Father

JEANNE D'ARC

PROLOGUE
For a thousand years from Rome to Aglncourt
Terror and darkness overspread the world
With superstition, bigotry, and crime,
While warring nations and marauding kings
Raven and slay and wither into dust.

Chivalry rides upon Its last crusade,
And Learning slumbers in the Church's tomb.
Barons and bishops, emperors and serfs,
Wallow In witchcraft, cruelty, and greed,
As if the angels had forgotten earth.

Hardly a voice to keep God's name alive;
Tin on a summer morn in lovely France,
On the shadowy forest border of the Vosges,
In small Domremy of peasant folk is born

A Little Sister of the Nazarene.

Music

CHORUS
Who remembers God's poor
In their humble attire?
Yet In them shall endure
The seed and the fire, —
The strength for fulfilment of longings, and faith for the dreaming of dreams.

Who stands with rapt gaze
In a day-dream, and sees, —
While her quiet sheep graze
By the tall poplar trees, —
A shadowy legion advancing, an army that musters and gleams?

As a clear minster bell
Thrills the soul of the air,
Her voice lays a spell
O'er a realm in despair,
Till the laggard take arms at her summons, assured that God's champion is there.

In war-harness bright.
Through the dust and the fray,
With valor alight,
She forges her way,
Till her mission's victorious standard on the wind above Orleans streams.

No witchcraft was here, —
Slander wide of the mark!
Revelation shone clear
In the sainted Jeanne d'Arc, —
A strain of intrepid conviction, which greatly foresees and redeems.

[Outside Jacques d' Arc's home in the village of Domremy on the border of a great forest, **JEANNE** stands leaning against a tree a little away from the house. Her **FATHER** sits on a stone nearby. He is a peasant of the soil, already beginning to be old, and his mind is on the past. There is a stream with a few pollarded willows leaning over it not far away, and sheep are grazing in the meadow. It is near sundown on a summer day. A large pale moon is seen just rising over the wood. Subdued music is faintly heard through **JEANNE'S** speeches.

JEANNE
Father, I hear the voices now.
Canst thou not hear them, too, —
There by the forest edge, so clear,
So wonderful, so true,
With sound as sweet as the summer rain

When the little leaves are new?

HER FATHER
Ay, lass, I hear. 'Twill be the wind
Talking among the trees.
'Tis like a human voice, the wind,
Full of old melodies.
It minds me of the night I took
Thy mother on my knees.

JEANNE
Father, I cannot mind my work,
The voices call me so;
They call me at the dead of noon
When all the winds are low.
And when the golden dawn comes up
With not a breath to blow.

I hear them while I turn my wheel,
And while I tend my sheep;
I hear them in the dewy dusk
When I He down to sleep;
And even at the Holy Mass
My mind I cannot keep.

They call and call, 'Jehan, Jehan,
Thy harried country save!'
I hear them through the music's sound.
And when the censers wave.
As the procession of the Host
Goes up the minster nave.

HER FATHER
Ay, ay, I hear thee, lass, — I hear.
Thou mind'st me of my prime.
When I would go across the fields
In the eager summer time,
To court thy mother at her wheel,
Singing an eerie rhymie.

She always had the misty look
Of things unkenned and far;
And always fancies in her head
Of princes, rhymes, and war, —
And how the Little People dance
Around the evening star. . . .

Midsummer Eve It was. I mind

There was a smell of bloom;
Out of the dusk a little wind
Went whispering through the room;
And all the meadow was alive
With fireflies in the gloom.

JEANNE
Father, I see the Figure now.
'Tis St. Michael with his sword,
And a great white shield on his arm.
He marches to award
Her rightful victory to France,
And I can hear his word.

HER FATHER
It Is the great shield of the moon
That Is so bright and round.
It is the mist from off the stream.
That moves along the ground.
As quiet as a churchyard ghost
That never makes a sound.

JEANNE
'And there Is Merlin In his cloak
Who comes to counsel me,
That since a wanton ruined France,
A maid must set her free.
'Jehan, rejoice, God's holy choice
Has fallen on Domremy'.

HER FATHER
'Tis but the crooked willow bole,
That leans across the brook.
The long grey moss Is like a beard.
He has an ancient look.
I've often marked him leaning there,
Like a shepherd on his crook.

JEANNE
Father, I see our banners pass;
The horses strain and neigh;
Our men at arms in cavalcade.
And knights in war array.
And kings and squires with commoners
Are hasting to the fray.

And at their head in whitest mall,
A standard in her hand,

Whereon the Virgin sits enthroned
And fair white lilies stand,
Rides thy Jehan, for serving man,
To free her luckless land.

Rank upon rank with dust and clank
The fuming chargers go.
Our halberds gleam, our pennons stream,
The level spears are low,
On helm and lance the sunbeams dance. . . .
I would I need not go!

HER FATHER
Ay, ay! Thy mother had these flights.
I mind her fancies well.
Sometimes she'd hear a cry for help,
Times an alarum bell.
And times in the half-dusk she'd see
Strange sights she would not tell.

I mind the night I brought her home
They seemed to vex her sore.
She had a fey look on her face,
When I led her through the door.
But when the good God sent thee down,
Ghosts troubled her no more.

When thou art wed and far this place,
'Twin mend, my lass, 'twill mend, —
When thou hast daughters by the hand.
And a man-child to tend!
For God himself sets store by love,
And love is dreamlng's end.

JEANNE
Father, you do not understand.
The only love I ask
Is Christ and his dear Mother's love.
To aid me in my task.
And send the French swords ringing down
Through English shield and casque.

So I must seek my lord the King,
And be his counsellor, —
Tell him the angel's messages
That bid him forth to war.
And I must ride, as his maiden guide,
Though I should die therefor.

The voices of the ancient wood
Have put the power on me.
The angels summon Jehan d'Arc
To serve God's destiny.
For pity on the realm of France. . . .
But what am I to thee?

[At this the **OLD MAN** rises from his seat. It is his only sign of feeling so far.

HER FATHER
How should a maid go to the wars,
With rough-shod men to ride?
Be there no captains near the King,
To counsel and to guide?
Is there no doubt of this thy call?
Must we this ill abide?

What dost thou say? What art to me?
My own lass! God thee keep! . . .

[Embracing her, he turns to brush away tears.

It Is the mist among the trees.
Go now and fold thy sheep I . . .

[He sits wearily.

It is the mist upon the plain.
I am weary unto sleep I

[His head sinks forward on his breast. His hands lie idle. In the fading daylight **JEANNE** stands gazing into the dusk.

Curtain and Music

IX.

VITTORIA COLONNA

1535 A. D.

PERSONS IN THE SCENE
VITTORIA COLONNA

MICHELANGELO
Two LADIES

PROLOGUE

When rash Columbus sailed Into the West
Following the sun beyond the unknown seas,
And beached his prows upon a fair New World,
Another realm was rising from the deeps
Of troubled faith and mediaeval night.

In the glad morning of the Renaissance,
After long sleep, the holy spirit of man
Awoke once more to learning, freedom, art.
Out of decrepit creeds belief arose
To seek more seemly garments for the soul.

Erasmus, Luther, Raphael and the rest,
Would build again in the sun of natural joy
The House of Life long mouldering in the shade.
And who now should the master builder be,
But the fiery seraph, Michelangelo?

Music

CHORUS
Who stands in the sun
By the dark cypress wall,
In scarlet and dun,
Where the autumn leaves fall, —
In a halo of shining hair, like a missal saint aureoled?

Is she empress or queen,
With that confident heart,
And her robes' silken sheen
As they flutter and part?
What wrong would not right in her presence?
What eye could its homage withhold?

Her rare jewels glance.
Her linked girdle slips.
With each turn of the dance
To flash and eclipse.
As she moves through an eloquent measure, with an old Latin song on her lips.

Her eyes have the light
Of the knowledge of truth.
As ancient as night,
As guileless as youth,
And glad as the rose-lidded morning new-risen, yet centuries old.

What gift could Time bring
To Learning's Re-birth,
As welcome as spring
When It visits the earth?
One flower, Vittoria Colonna, red lily with deep heart of gold!

[A secluded part of the gardens of the Colonna Palace in Rome, a square of smooth green turf surrounded by a tall clipped cypress hedge. There is a flat marble bench at the back, and a bushy golden-tipped cedar, about three feet high, in each corner of the enclosure. There is only one entrance through the hedge, at the left, guarded on either side by two termini, antique marble posts with sculptured heads, a Pan on the left, a Hermes on the right. As the curtain rises **VITTORIA COLONNA** is discovered, moving through a slow ballade, and singing a Mediaval Latin student song as an accompaniment. Two companions, or **SERVING-WOMEN**, stand by, an appreciative audience of her performance.

Song
When the pear tree comes in flower,
Cold and grief are gone away,
Love and gladness have their hour.
Amor vincit omnia!

When the leaves begin to fall.
Youth and spring have had their day,
Why should lovers fear at all?
Amor vincit omnia!

[As she begins the second stanza, a man's **VOICE** is heard outside joining in the song. The **WOMEN** smile, as if not surprised, and presently there enters one who is evidently a welcome and accustomed guest of the house. It is **MICHELANGELO**. As he comes in, without interrupting the dance, he smiles and bows in courteous mock-stilted salutation, and takes his stand by the Hermes until the stanza is finished. Then he advances, and as he takes **VITTORIA COLONNA'S** hand, leads her to the bench.

[She sits at one end of the seat, while he remains standing near the other. The waiting **WOMEN** retire. It is afternoon of a warm, still day in autumn.

VITTORIA COLONNA
Did they dance such things in Florence,
In that Medicean garden,
Where magnificent Lorenzo
Crowned your toil with praise or pardon?
When that young faun's head you fashioned,
Was his voice enough to fire you?
Were there not within the cloister

Other accents to inspire you?

Buonarroti, how this New Life,
Just as every hope seemed ended,
Breaking on us like a vision.
Makes the old more rich and splendid! —
As, how often at the casement
I have watched through storm and thunder,
Till at last the sudden rain ceased
And the sun showed Rome in wonder!l

So when all our age seemed darkest,
Faith extinguished, culture perished.
Comes a Renaissance of Knowledge,
Freeing all the dreams we cherished.
All the lore of buried Hellas
Brought to light for our illuming!
On old altars reared to Beauty
Burn once more the fires consuming!

Who can walk unmoved through Florence,
Where each corner shows a palace?
Who but must learn adoration
From the chasing on the chalice?
Who could meanly live, with Dante
Ringing through his soul's dim portals?
Or be sad where Lippo Lippi
Paints the teeming life of mortals.

What if here, as once in Athens,
Women now should lift the story
Of our race from prose to epic.
With new freedom, grace, and glory!
We should walk the world like morning
On the hill-tops dark and olden,
When the sombre peaks of purple
Glow transfigured fresh and golden;

Sane and lofty as Athene,
Yet with laughter, fire, and daring;
And deep-bosomed as Demeter
When she had the earth in caring.
So shall time's victorious children
Reach the height and pass the portal
Of that majesty of beauty
Thou hast Imaged — more than mortal.

All thy life long, Michelangel.

Thou hast fought the dull and downward, —
Followed only where truth pointed.
While the many trailed renownward.
Where great arches lift to heaven
The dumb heart of the observer,
Caught In color, pressed in marble.
Live thy dreams, thy faith, thy fervor.

All that thou hast wrought of beauty.
Framed or fashioned, In the hour
Of God's counsel, stands forever
To uplift this world with power.
Strong old prophets, wise young princes,
Moses, David, dear Madonna,
All In thy great heart have portion.
What am I to thee?

MICHELANGELO
Colonna!
Never that note of despairing sadness,
Of human tears and sublime regret!
Keep ever thy voice of seraph's gladness,
Lest time should lose and the world forget
The image of joy no man can measure, —
Transcending nature, surpassing art, —
The eternal dream, the immortal treasure,
The flower that blows in a woman's heart!

Here stand we, while the great sky arches
Blue over Rome, triumphal, sheer;
And Autumn with banner and vestment marches
In festal pomp for the dying year.
What is this earth but a minster old
The wind like a crowding organ fills.
Where the sun swings up like a censer of gold
Before the high altar of the hills? . . .

Suppose from out of the world somewhere
Into a great dim church should stray
An untaught urchin, unaware
Whose house it is, what It means to pray;
He wanders on where the soaring nave
Goes up and up, and the soft light falls,
Where faded colors are marshalled brave,
Row on row o'er the choir stalls.

The marble knights that sleep so still,
The saints that stand in their carven screen,

The gargoyles each with a different thrill, —
What do the manifold marvels mean?
And ever as the wonder grows.
Assurance and daring begin to fall,
Until where the great east window glows,
He halts abashed by the chancel rail.

And there before the altar stands,
To steady the faint heart's come-and-go,
An angel with lily-laden hands,
Smiling down on the boy below. . . .
I was that venturesome child, and thou —
Who but the angel great and fair,
With the all-seeing eyes, the unanxious brow.
The curved sweet mouth, and the luminous hair!

As all of a sudden the world will glow
In the first bright single shaft of dawn,
Or the wonder of a painting grow
When the scaffold Is down and the screen withdrawn,
I caught at last the soul of design,
The might of color, the reason of form,
The magic of rhythm and melting line.
When you moved like music alive and warm.

I saw where enchanted Beauty slept,
Like the Fairy Princess, In color and stone,
Till forth at the prayer of my hand she leapt
Into a kingdom long her own.
Onward I blundered, with heart uplift.
To prove, — the only faith I knew, —
That mould of body reveals soul's drift.
I dreamed my dreams, and lo, they are true!—

Therefore, I say, regret no more!
Shall the strong man grieve for his callow prime.
When autumn and triumph are at the door.
And labor and love are lords of time?
Thou art the April of Angelo, —
Thine untarnished smiles, thy generous tears!
What does the heavenly lilac know
Of the falling leaves and the flying years?

This evergreen with golden tip!
Be that our emblem treasured fast,
As if to remind us, finger on lip,
Endure and essay! Truth wins at last!
When the earth is judged of good and ill.

And men at the Mercy Seat shall stand.
As I love you now, I shall love you still.
Great heart, in homage I kiss your hand!

[As he bends over one hand, **VITTORIA COLONNA** lays the other, half playfully, half affectionately, on his head, and, as he rises, leads him through a figure of her ballade, while they sing together a final stanza of her song.

Song
Let the winter come with snow.
Iron ground and skies of grey, —
What to high hearts, whether or no?
Amor vincit omnia!

[With the concluding passage of the dance, they go out through the high hedge hand in hand, and the singing fades in the distance.

Curtain and Music

EPILOGUE AND CLOSING CHORUS

PERSONS IN THE EPILOGUE AND CLOSING CHORUS
TIME
A POET
MODERN WOMAN

EPILOGUE
Ye have beheld in art's transporting glass
Some portion of the pageantry of Time
Moving across the vast stage of the world,
And marked in power and in beauty there
Wondrous earth women with the gift of life.

Indomitable children of the light,
Impassioned with high themes of endless good,
They bore the subtle and Immortal hope, —
The magic seed that should transmute this earth
Into a paradise where gods might dwell.

Look forth upon the modern world and see
The same great being passionate and fair.
Charged with her mystic wisdom as of old.
Still championing the sorcery of love

And the ecstatic progress of the Soul!

Music

[As the curtain rises for the closing chorus **MODERN WOMAN** is seen standing in the foreground, with a shadowy multitude behind her, in which the figures of **VITTORIA COLONNA**, **JEANNE d'ARC**, **ZENOBIA**, **MARY**, **IZEYL**, **SAPPHO**, **BALKIS**, **DEBORAH**, and **EVE** can be distinguished.

CLOSING CHORUS
Who is here through the hush
Of the infinite past,
With the confident gush
Of spring come at last,
As youth must arise from all sorrow to share in the triumph of earth?

In her hair the gold light
Of the sun when day dies.
And the violet night
In her dusk-lidded eyes.
With the freshness of dew in her bearing, and morn in her stature and girth!

Her throat is unlaced.
Her foot is soft-shod;
She is glad and free-paced
As the creatures of God;
Her way is the path to perfection her sisters of morning have trod.

With the ardor of Eve
And Zenobla's pride,
She Is quick to believe,
With soul for her guide;
She could go forth with Barak to battle, or grace Jehan's corselet of mall.

Was Sappho more tender,
Colonna more wise?
Does Mary not lend her
Great motherhood's guise?
She is soft with the beauty of Balkis, sublime with the love of Izeyl.

With solace and fire,
With dawn in her voice,
She lives to inspire.
Companion, rejoice, —
A presence of radiant devotion, a spirit of luminous choice.

Have ye felt the heart quail
And uplift and hold fast,
At the swell of the sail

As It pulls on the mast?
Even so must the sway of her being empower the world to the last.

Curtain and Music

Bliss Carman - An Appreciation

How many Canadians—how many even among the few who seek to keep themselves informed of the best in contemporary literature, who are ever on the alert for the new voices—realise, or even suspect, that this Northern land of theirs has produced a poet of whom it may be affirmed with confidence and assurance that he is of the great succession of English poets? Yet such—strange and unbelievable though it may seem—is in very truth the case, that poet being (to give him his full name) William Bliss Carman. Canada has full right to be proud of her poets, a small body though they are; but not only does Mr. Carman stand high and clear above them all—his place (and time cannot but confirm and justify the assertion) is among those men whose poetry is the shining glory of that great English literature which is our common heritage.

If any should ask why, if what has been just said is so, there has been—as must be admitted—no general recognition of the fact in the poet's home land, I would answer that there are various and plausible, if not good, reasons for it.

First of all, the poet, as thousands more of our young men of ambition and confidence have done, went early to the United States, and until recently, except for rare and brief visits to his old home down by the sea, has never returned to Canada—though for all that, I am able to state, on his own authority, he is still a Canadian citizen. Then all his books have had their original publication in the United States, and while a few of them have subsequently carried the imprints of Canadian publishers, none of these can be said ever to have made any special effort to push their sale. Another reason for the fact above mentioned is that Mr. Carman has always scorned to advertise himself, while his work has never been the subject of the log-rolling and booming which the work of many another poet has had—to his ultimate loss. A further reason is that he follows a rule of his own in preparing his books for publication. Most poets publish a volume of their work as soon as, through their industry and perseverance, they have material enough on hand to make publication desirable in their eyes. Not so with Mr. Carman, however, his rule being not to publish until he has done sufficient work of a certain general character or key to make a volume. As a result, you cannot fully know or estimate his work by one book, or two books, or even half a dozen; you must possess or be familiar with every one of the score and more volumes which contain his output of poetry before you can realise how great and how many-sided is his genius.

It is a common remark on the part of those who respond readily to the vigorous work of Kipling, or Masefield, even our own Service, that Bliss Carman's poetry has no relation to or concern with ordinary, everyday life. One would suppose that most persons who cared for poetry at all turned to it as a relief from or counter to the burdens and vexations of the daily round; but in any event, the remark referred to seems to me to indicate either the most casual acquaintance with Mr. Carman's work, or a complete misunderstanding and misapprehension of the meaning of it. I grant that you will find little or nothing in it all to remind you of the grim realities and vexing social problems of this modern existence of ours; but to say or to suggest that these things do not exist for Mr. Carman is to say or to suggest something which is the reverse of true. The truth is, he is aware of them as only one with the sensitive organism of a poet can be; but he does not feel that he has a call or mission to remedy them, and still less to sing of them. He therefore leaves the immediate problems of the day to those who choose, or are led, to occupy themselves therewith, and turns resolutely away to dwell upon those things which for him possess infinitely greater importance.

"What are they?" one who knows Mr. Carman only as, say, a lyrist of spring or as a singer of the delights of vagabondia probably will ask in some wonder. Well, the things which concern him above all, I would answer, are first, and naturally, the beauty and wonder of this world of ours, and next the mystery of the earthly pilgrimage of the human soul out of eternity and back into it again.

The poems in the present volume—which, by the way, can boast the high honor of being the very first regular Canadian edition of his work—will be evidence ample and conclusive to every reader, I am sure, of the place which

The perennial enchanted
Lovely world and all its lore

occupy in the heart and soul of Bliss Carman, as well as of the magical power with which he is able to convey the deep and unfailing satisfaction and delight which they possess for him. They, however, represent his latest period (he has had three well-defined periods), comprising selections from three of his last published volumes: The Rough Rider, Echoes from Vagabondia, and April Airs, together with a number of new poems, and do not show, except here and there and by hints and flashes, how great is his preoccupation with the problem of man's existence—

—the hidden import
Of man's eternal plight.

This is manifest most in certain of his earlier books, for in these he turns and returns to the greatest of all the problems of man almost constantly, probing, with consummate and almost unrivalled use of the art of expression, for the secret which surely, he clearly feels, lies hidden somewhere, to be discovered if one could but pierce deeply enough. Pick up Behind the Arras, and as you turn over page after page you cannot but observe how incessantly the poet's mind—like the minds of his two great masters, Browning and Whitman—works at this problem. In "Behind the Arras," the title poem; "In the Wings," "The Crimson House," "The Lodger," "Beyond the Gamut," "The Juggler"—yes, in every poem in the book—he takes up and handles the strange thing we know as, or call, life, turning it now this way, now that, in an effort to find out its meaning and purpose. He comes but little nearer success in this than do most of the rest of men, of course; but the magical and ever-fresh beauty of his expression, the haunting melody of his lines, the variety of his images and figures and the depth and range of his thought, put his searchings and ponderings in a class by themselves.

Lengthy quotation from Mr. Carman's books is not permitted here, and I must guide myself accordingly, though with reluctance, because I believe that in a study such as this the subject should be allowed to speak for himself as much as possible. In "Behind the Arras" the poet describes the passage from life to death as

A cadence dying down unto its source
In music's course,

and goes on to speak of death as

—the broken rhythm of thought and man,
The sweep and span
Of memory and hope
About the orbit where they still must grope
For wider scope,

To be through thousand springs restored, renewed,
With love imbrued,
With increments of will
Made strong, perceiving unattainment still
From each new skill.

Now follow some verses from "Behind the Gamut," to my mind the poet's greatest single achievement;

As fine sand spread on a disc of silver,
At some chord which bids the motes combine,
Heeding the hidden and reverberant impulse,
Shifts and dances into curve and line,

The round earth, too, haply, like a dust-mote,
Was set whirling her assigned sure way,
Round this little orb of her ecliptic
To some harmony she must obey.

And what of man?

Linked to all his half-accomplished fellows,
Through unfrontiered provinces to range—
Man is but the morning dream of nature,
Roused to some wild cadence weird and strange.

Here, now, are some verses from "Pulvis et Umbra," which is to be found in Mr. Carman's first book, Low Tide on Grand Pré, and in which the poet addresses a moth which a storm has blown into his window:

For man walks the world with mourning
Down to death and leaves no trace,
With the dust upon his forehead,
And the shadow on his face.

Pillared dust and fleeing shadow
As the roadside wind goes by,
And the fourscore years that vanish
In the twinkling of an eye.

"Pillared dust and fleeing shadow." Where in all our English literature will one find the life history of man summed up more briefly and, at the same time, more beautifully, than in that wonderful line? Now follows a companion verse to those just quoted, taken from "Lord of My Heart's Elation," which stands in the forefront of From the Green Book of the Bards. It may be remarked here that while the poet recurs again and again to some favorite thought or idea, it is never in the same words. His expression is always new and fresh, showing how deep and true is his inspiration. Again it is man who is pictured:

A fleet and shadowy column
Of dust and mountain rain,
To walk the earth a moment
And be dissolved again.

But while Mr. Carman's speculations upon life's meaning and the mystery of the future cannot but appeal to the thoughtful-minded, it is as an interpreter of nature that he makes his widest appeal. Bliss Carman, I must say here, and emphatically, is no mere landscape-painter; he never, or scarcely ever, paints a picture of nature for its own sake. He goes beyond the outward aspect of things and interprets or translates for us with less keen senses as only a poet whose feeling for nature is of the deepest and profoundest, who has gone to her whole-heartedly and been taken close to her warm bosom, can do. Is this not evident from these verses from "The Great Return"—originally called "The Pagan's Prayer," and for some inscrutable reason to be found only in the limited Collected Poems, issued in two stately volumes in 1905.

When I have lifted up my heart to thee,
Thou hast ever hearkened and drawn near,
And bowed thy shining face close over me,
Till I could hear thee as the hill-flowers hear.

When I have cried to thee in lonely need,
Being but a child of thine bereft and wrung,
Then all the rivers in the hills gave heed;
And the great hill-winds in thy holy tongue—

That ancient incommunicable speech—
The April stars and autumn sunsets know—
Soothed me and calmed with solace beyond reach
Of human ken, mysterious and low.

Who can read or listen to those moving lines without feeling that Mr. Carman is in very truth a poet of nature—nay, Nature's own poet? But how could he be other when, in "The Breath of the Reed" (From the Green Book of the Bards), he makes the appeal?

Make me thy priest, O Mother,
And prophet of thy mood,
With all the forest wonder
Enraptured and imbued.

As becomes such a poet, and particularly a poet whose birth-month is April, Mr. Carman sings much of the early spring. Again and again he takes up his woodland pipe, and lo! Pan himself and all his train troop joyously before us. Yet the singer's notes for all his singing never become wearied or strident; his airs are ever new and fresh; his latest songs are no less spontaneous and winning than were his first, written how many years ago, while at the same time they have gained in beauty and melody. What heart will not stir to the vibrant music of his immortal "Spring Song," which was originally published in the first Songs from Vagabondia, and the opening verses of which follow?

Make me over, mother April,
When the sap begins to stir!
When thy flowery hand delivers
All the mountain-prisoned rivers,
And thy great heart beats and quivers
To revive the days that were,
Make me over, mother April,
When the sap begins to stir!

Take my dust and all my dreaming,
Count my heart-beats one by one,
Send them where the winters perish;
Then some golden noon recherish
And restore them in the sun,
Flower and scent and dust and dreaming,
With their heart-beats every one!

That poem is sufficient in itself to prove that Bliss Carman has full right and title to be called Spring's own lyrist, though it may be remarked here that not all his spring poems are so unfeignedly joyous. Many of them indeed, have a touch, or more than a touch, of wistfulness, for the poet knows well that sorrow lurks under all joy, deep and well hidden though it may be.

Mr. Carman sings equally finely, though perhaps not so frequently, of summer and the other seasons; but as he has other claims upon our attention, I shall forbear to labor the fact, particularly as the following collection demonstrates it sufficiently. One of those other claims is as a writer of sea poetry. Few poets, it may be said, have pictured the majesty and the mystery, the beauty and the terror of the sea, better than he. His Ballads of Lost Haven is a veritable treasure-house for those whose spirits find kinship in wide expanses of moving waters. One of the best known poems in this volume is "The Gravedigger," which opens thus:

Oh, the shambling sea is a sexton old,
And well his work is done.
With an equal grave for lord and knave,
He buries them every one.

Then hoy and rip, with a rolling hip,
He makes for the nearest shore;
And God, who sent him a thousand ship,
Will send him a thousand more;
But some he'll save for a bleaching grave,
And shoulder them in to shore—
Shoulder them in, shoulder them in,

Shoulder them in to shore.

In "The City of the Sea" (Last Songs from Vagabondia) Mr. Carman speaks of the seabells sounding

The eternal cadence of sea sorrow
For Man's lot and immemorial wrong—
The lost strains that haunt the human dwelling
With the ghost of song.

Elsewhere he speaks of

The great sea, mystic and musical.

And here from another poem is a striking picture:

... the old sea
Seems to whimper and deplore
Mourning like a childless crone
With her sorrow left alone—
The eternal human cry
To the heedless passer-by.

I have said above that Mr. Carman has had three distinct periods, and intimated that the poems in the following collection are of his third period. The first period may be said to be represented by the Low Tide and Behind the Arras volumes, while the second is displayed in the three volumes of Songs from Vagabondia, which he published in association with his friend Richard Hovey. Bliss Carman was from the first too original and individual a poet to be directly influenced by anyone else; but there can be no doubt that his friendship with Hovey helped to turn him from over-preoccupation with mysteries which, for all their greatness, are not for man to solve, to an intenser realisation of the beauty and loveliness of the world about him and of the joys of human fellowship. The result is seen in such poems as "Spring Song," quoted in part above, and his perhaps equally well-known "The Joys of the Road," which appeared in the same volume with that poem, and a few verses from which follow:

Now the joys of the road are chiefly these:
A crimson touch on the hardwood trees;

A vagrant's morning wide and blue,
In early fall, when the wind walks, too;

A shadowy highway cool and brown,
Alluring up and enticing down

From rippled waters and dappled swamp,
From purple glory to scarlet pomp;

The outward eye, the quiet will,
And the striding heart from hill to hill.

Some of the finest of arman's work is contained in his elegiac or memorial poems, in which he commemorates Keats, Shelley, William Blake, Lincoln, Stevenson, and other men for whom he has a kindred feeling, and also friends whom he has loved and lost. Listen to these moving lines from "Non Omnis Moriar," written in memory of Gleeson White, and to be found in Last Songs from Vagabondia:

There is a part of me that knows,
Beneath incertitude and fear,
I shall not perish when I pass
Beyond mortality's frontier;

But greatly having joyed and grieved,
Greatly content, shall hear the sigh
Of the strange wind across the lone
Bright lands of taciturnity.

In patience therefore I await
My friend's unchanged benign regard,—
Some April when I too shall be
Spilt water from a broken shard.

In "The White Gull," written for the centenary of the birth of Shelley in 1892, and included in By the Aurelian Wall, he thus apostrophizes that clear and shining spirit:

O captain of the rebel host,
Lead forth and far!
Thy toiling troopers of the night
Press on the unavailing fight;
The sombre field is not yet lost,
With thee for star.

Thy lips have set the hail and haste
Of clarions free
To bugle down the wintry verge
Of time forever, where the surge
Thunders and trembles on a waste
And open sea.

In "A Seamark," a threnody for Robert Louis Stevenson, which appears in the same volume, the poet hails "R.L.S." (of whose tribe he may be said to be truly one) as

The master of the roving kind,

and goes on:

O all you hearts about the world
In whom the truant gypsy blood,
Under the frost of this pale time,
Sleeps like the daring sap and flood

That dreams of April and reprieve!
You whom the haunted vision drives,
Incredulous of home and ease.
Perfection's lovers all your lives!

You whom the wander-spirit loves
To lead by some forgotten clue
Forever vanishing beyond
Horizon brinks forever new;
Our restless loved adventurer,
On secret orders come to him,
Has slipped his cable, cleared the reef,
And melted on the white sea-rim.

"Perfection's lovers all your lives." Of these, it may be said without qualification, is Bliss Carman himself.

No summary of Mr. Carman's work, however cursory, would be worthy of the name if it omitted mention of his ventures in the realm of Greek myth. From the Book of Myths is made up of work of that sort, every poem in it being full of the beauty of phrase and melody of which Mr. Carman alone has the secret. The finest poems in the book, barring the opening one, "Overlord," are "Daphne," "The Dead Faun," "Hylas," and "At Phædra's Tomb," but I can do no more here than name them, for extracts would fail to reveal their full beauty. And beauty, after all is said, is the first and last thing with Mr. Carman. As he says himself somewhere:

The joy of the hand that hews for beauty
Is the dearest solace under the sun.

And again

The eternal slaves of beauty
Are the masters of the world.

A slave—a happy, willing slave—to beauty is the poet himself, and the world can never repay him for the message of beauty which he has brought it.

Kindred to From the Book of Myths, but much more important, is Sappho: One Hundred Lyrics, one of the most successful of the numerous attempts which have been made to recapture the poems by that high priestess of song which remain to us only in fragments. Mr. Carman, as Charles G. D. Roberts points out in an introduction to the volume, has made no attempt here at translation or paraphrasing; his venture has been "the most perilous and most alluring in the whole field of poetry"—that of imaginative and, at the same time, interpretive construction. Brief quotation again would fail to convey an adequate idea of the exquisiteness of the work, and all I can do, therefore, is to urge all lovers of real poetry to possess themselves of Sappho: One Hundred Lyrics, for it is literally a storehouse of lyric beauty.

I must not fail here to speak of From the Book of Valentines, which contains some lovely things, notably "At the Great Release." This is not only one of the finest of all Mr. Carman's poems, but it is also one of the finest poems of our time. It is a love poem, and no one possessing any real feeling for poetry can read it without experiencing that strange thrill of the spirit which only the highest form of poetry can communicate. "Morning and Evening," "In an Iris Meadow," and "A letter from Lesbos" must be also mentioned. In the last named poem, Sappho is represented as writing to Gorgo, and expresses herself in these moving words:

If the high gods in that triumphant time
Have calendared no day for thee to come
Light-hearted to this doorway as of old,
Unmoved I shall behold their pomps go by—
The painted seasons in their pageantry,
The silvery progressions of the moon,
And all their infinite ardors unsubdued,
Pass with the wind replenishing the earth

Incredulous forever I must live
And, once thy lover, without joy behold,
The gradual uncounted years go by,
Sharing the bitterness of all things made.

Mention must be now made of Songs of the Sea Children, which can be described only as a collection of the sweetest and tenderest love lyrics written in our time—

—the lyric songs
The earthborn children sing,
When wild-wood laughter throngs
The shy bird-throats of spring;
When there's not a joy of the heart
But flies like a flag unfurled,
And the swelling buds bring back
The April of the world.

So perfect and complete are these lyrics that it would be almost sacrilege to quote any of them unless entire. Listen however, to these verses:

The day is lost without thee,
The night has not a star.
Thy going is an empty room
Whose door is left ajar.

Depart: it is the footfall
Of twilight on the hills.
Return: and every rood of ground
Breaks into daffodils.

There are those who will have it that Bliss Carman has been away from Canada so long that he has ceased to be, in a real sense, a Canadian. Such assume rather than know, for a very little study of his work would show them that it is shot through and through with the poet's feeling for the land of his birth. Memories of his childhood and youthful years down by the sea are still fresh in Mr. Carman's mind, and inspire him again and again in his writing. "A Remembrance," at the beginning of the present collection, may be pointed to as a striking instance of this, but proof positive is the volume, Songs from a Northern Garden, for it could have been written only by a Canadian, born and bred, one whose heart and soul thrill to the thought of Canada. I would single out from this volume for special mention as being "Canadian" in the fullest sense "In a Grand Pré Garden," "The Keeper's Silence," "At Home and Abroad," "Killoleet," and "Above the Gaspereau," but have no space to quote from them.

But Mr. Carman is not only a Canadian, he is also a Briton; and evidence of this is his Ode on the Coronation, written on the occasion of the crowning of King Edward VII in 1902. This poem—the very existence of which is hardly known among us—ought to be put in the hands of every child and youth who speaks the English tongue, for no other, I dare maintain—nothing by Kipling, or Newbolt, or any other of our so-called "Imperial singers"—expresses more truly and more movingly the deep feeling of love and reverence which the very thought of England evokes in every son of hers, even though it may never have been his to see her white cliffs rise or to tread her storied ground:

O England, little mother by the sleepless Northern tide,
Having bred so many nations to devotion, trust, and pride,
Very tenderly we turn
With welling hearts that yearn
Still to love you and defend you,—let the sons of men discern
Wherein your right and title, might and majesty, reside.

In concluding this, I greatly fear, lamentably inadequate study, I come to the collection which follows, and which, as intimated above, represents the work of Mr. Carman's latest period. I must say at once that, while I yield to no one in admiration for Low Tide and the other books of that period, or for the work of the second period, as represented by the Songs from Vagabondia volumes, I have no hesitation in declaring that I regard the poet's work of the past few years with even higher admiration. It may not possess the force and vigor of the work which preceded it; but anything seemingly missing in that respect is more than made up for me by increased beauty and clarity of expression. The mysticism—verging, or more than verging, at times on symbolism—which marked his earlier poems, and which hung, as it were, as a veil between them and the reader, has gone, and the poet's thought or theme now lies clearly before us as in a mirror. What—to take a verse from the following pages at random—could be more pellucid, more crystal clear in expression—what indeed, could come closer to that achieving of the impossible at which every real poet must aim—than this from "In Gold Lacquer".

Gold are the great trees overhead,
And gold the leaf-strewn grass,
As though a cloth of gold were spread
To let a seraph pass.
And where the pageant should go by,
Meadow and wood and stream,
The world is all of lacquered gold,
Expectant as a dream.

The poet, happily, has fully recovered from the serious illness which laid him low some two years ago, and which for a time caused his friends and admirers the gravest concern, and so we may look forward hopefully to seeing further volumes of verse come from the press to make certain his name and fame.

But if, for any reason, this should not be—which the gods forfend!—Later Poems, I dare affirm, must and will be regarded as the fine flower and crowning achievement of the genius and art of Bliss Carman.

R. H. HATHAWAY.
Toronto, 1921.

Bliss Carman – A Short Biography

William Bliss Carman was born in Fredericton, in New Brunswick on April 15th 1861. 'Bliss' was his mother's maiden name. She was descended from Daniel Bliss of Concord, Massachusetts, who was the great-grandfather to Ralph Waldo Emerson.

Carman was educated at Fredericton Collegiate School. Here, under the influence of the headmaster George Robert Parkin, he gained an appreciation of classical literature and was introduced to the poetry of many of the Pre-Raphaelites especially Dante Gabriel Rossetti and Algernon Charles Swinburne.

From here he graduated to the University of New Brunswick, obtaining his B.A. there in 1881. As is common with so many writers his first published piece was for the University magazine and for Carman that was in 1879.

England now beckoned and he spent a year at Oxford and then the University of Edinburgh (1882–1883). He returned home to Canada to work on his M.A. which he obtained from the University of New Brunswick in 1884.

Tragically his father died in January, 1885, followed by his mother in February of the following year. Carman now enrolled in Harvard University for a year. There he met and was part of a literary circle that included the American poet Richard Hovey, who would become his close friend, and later collaborator, on the successful Vagabondia poetry series. Carman and Hovey were members of the "Visionists" circle along with Herbert Copeland and F. Holland Day, who would later form the Boston publishing firm Copeland & Day and, in turn, launch Vagabondia.

After Harvard Carman briefly returned to Canada, but was back in Boston by February of 1890 saying "Boston is one of the few places where my critical education and tastes could be of any use to me in earning money. New York and London are about the only other places." However, he was unable to find work in Boston but was more successful in New York becoming the literary editor of the semi-religious New York Independent. There he helped Canadian poets get published and introduced them to a wider readership than they could receive in Canada.

However, Carman and work as an editor were not destined for a long career together and he was dismissed in 1892. There followed short stays with Current Literature, Cosmopolitan, The Chap-Book, and The Atlantic Monthly. Whilst these appointments provided the basis for a career and an income he was not suited to their demands. From 1895 he would only work as a contributor to magazines and newspapers whilst he worked on his volumes of poetry.

Carman first published a book of poetry in 1893 with Low Tide on Grand Pré. He had written the title poem in the summer of 1886 and it had (whilst he was still at Harvard) been published in the spring of

1887 by Atlantic Monthly. Despite its critical acceptance there was no Canadian company prepared to publish the volume. When an American company did so it went bankrupt. Life was becoming difficult for the young poet.

The following year was decidedly better. His partnership with Richard Hovey had given birth to Songs of Vagabondia and it was published by their friends at Copeland & Day. It was an immediate success. The young men were delighted at such a reception. It quickly sold out and was re-printed a number of times. Although these re-prints were small (usually 500-1000 copies) they were frequent.

On the back of this success they would write a further three volumes, which in their turn were almost as successful. They quickly became the center of a cult following, especially among students who empathized with the poetry's anti-materialistic themes, its celebration of personal freedom, and its glorification of comradeship."

The success of Songs of Vagabondia prompted the Boston firm, Stone & Kimball, to reissue Low Tide on Grand Pré and to hire Carman as the editor of its literary journal, The Chapbook. This ceased after a year when the company relocated and Carman expressed his desire to remain in Boston.

In 1885 Carman brought out Behind the Arras, a somewhat more serious and philosophical work centered on the premise of a long meditation using the speaker's house and its many rooms as a symbol of life and the choices to be made. However, the idea and its execution did not quite meld.

Signficantly, in 1896, Carman met Mrs Mary Perry King, who rapidly became patron, adviser and sometime lover. She put money in his pocket, and food in his mouth and, when he struck bottom, often repaired his confidence as well as helping to sell the work. She also later became his writing collaborator on two verse dramas.

Mitchell Kennerley, Carman's roommate wrote that, "On the rare occasions they had intimate relations they always advised me of by leaving a bunch of violets — Mary favorite flower — on the pillow of my bed." If her husband, Dr. King, knew of this arrangement he seems not to have objected. He was a great supporter of Carman's career and seemingly his wife's complicated involvement with that.

In 1897 Carman published Ballad of Lost Haven, a collection of poetry about the sea. Its notable poems include the macabre sea shanty, The Gravedigger. The following year, 1898, came By the Aurelian Wall, the title poem itself was an elegy to John Keats and the book a collection of formal elegies.

In 1899 his publisher, Lamson, Wolffe was taken over by the Boston firm of Small, Maynard & Co., who had also acquired the rights to Low Tide on Grand Pré. The copyrights to of his books were now held by one publisher and, in lieu of earnings, Carman took what would ultimately be a disastrous financial stake in the company.

As the century turned Carman was hard at work on what would eventually be a five-volume set of poetry; "Pans Pipes". Pan, the goat-god, was traditionally associated with poetry and the coming together of the earthly and the divine. The five volumes were all published between 1902 – 1905.

The inspiration for this came from Mary who had persuaded Carman to write in both prose and poetry about the ideas of 'unitrinianism.' This drew on the theories of François-Alexandre-Nicolas-Chéri Delsarte and was defined as a strategy of mind-body-spirit harmonization aimed at undoing the physical, psychological, and spiritual damage caused by urban modernity. The definition may be rather woolly but for Carman it resulted in some very fine work across the five-volume series. This shared belief between Mary and Carman created a further bond but did isolate him from his circle of friends.

The excellence of a number of these poems did much to install Carman as the most noted of Canadian Poets and eventually their own Poet Laureate. Among the most often quoted and printed are "The Dead Faun" (from Volume I), "Lord of My Heart's Elation" (Volume II) and many of the erotic poems from Volume III.

In the middle of publication in 1903, Small, Maynard failed and with it went all the assets Carman had tied up in the company.

Carman immediately signed with another Boston publisher, L.C. Page, who would publish seven new books of Carman poetry in this hectic period up to 1905. They released a further three books based on Carman's Transcript columns, and a prose work on Unitrinianism, The Making of Personality, that he'd written with Mary King.

Carman now felt secure enough to pursue his 'dream project,' namely a deluxe edition of his collected poetry to 1903. Page acquired the distribution rights on the condition that the book be sold privately, by subscription. Unfortunately, the demand wasn't there and it failed. Carman was deeply disappointed and lost faith in Page. However, their grip on his copyrights was absolute and sadly no further collected editions were to be published during his lifetime.

By 1904 his income was restricted and the offer to be editor-in-chief of the 10-volume project, The World's Best Poetry, was eagerly accepted.

For Carman perhaps his best years as a poet were now behind him. From 1908 he lived near the Kings' New Canaan, Connecticut, estate, that he named "Sunshine", or in the summer in a cabin in the Catskills, which he called "Moonshine."

With Literary tastes now moving away from what he could provide his income further dwindled and his health started to deteriorate.

In 1912 Carman published the final work in the Vagabondia series. Richard Hovey had died in 1900 and so this last work was purely his. It has a distinct elegiac tone as if remembering the past works themselves.

Although Carman was not politically active he did campaign during the World War One, as a member of the Vigilantes, who supported the American entry into the titanic struggle on the Allied side.

By 1920, Carman was impoverished and recovering from a near-fatal attack of tuberculosis. He returned to Canada and began to undertake a series of publicly successful and somewhat lucrative reading tours, saying "there is nothing worth talking of in book sales compared with reading. Breathless attention, crowded halls, and a strange, profound enthusiasm such as I never guessed could be,' he reported to a friend. 'And good thrifty money too. Think of it! An entirely new life for me, and I am the most surprised person in Canada.'"

On October 28th, 1921 Carman was honored at a dinner held by the newly-formed Canadian Authors' Association, at the Ritz Carlton Hotel in Montreal, where he was crowned Canada's Poet Laureate with a wreath of maple leaves.

Carman is placed among the Confederation Poets, a group that included his cousin, Charles G.D. Roberts, Archibald Lampman, and Duncan Campbell Scott. Carman was perhaps the best and is credited with the widest recognition. However, whilst the others carefully supplemented their income with writing novels and works for the magazines, or even other careers, Carman only wrote poetry together with a small amount of writing on literary ideas, philosophy, and aesthetics.

He continued his reading tours, and by 1925 had finally secured a new Canadian publisher; McClelland & Stewart (Toronto), who issued a collection of selected earlier verse and would now became his main publisher. Although they benefited from Carman's increased popularity and his revered position in Canadian literature, his former publisher L.C. Page would not relinquish its copyrights to his earlier works.

In his last years, Carman was a member of the Halifax literary and social set, The Song Fishermen and in 1927 he edited The Oxford Book of American Verse.

William Bliss Carman died of a brain hemorrhage, at the age of 68, in New Canaan on the 8th June, 1929. He was cremated in New Canaan and his ashes interred at Forest Hill Cemetery, Fredericton, with a national memorial service held at the Anglican cathedral there.

It was only a quarter of a century later, on May 13th, 1954, that a scarlet maple tree was planted at his graveside, to honour his request in the 1892 poem "The Grave-Tree":

Let me have a scarlet maple
For the grave-tree at my head,
With the quiet sun behind it,
In the years when I am dead.

Bliss Carman – A Concise Bibliography

Poetry Collections
Low Tide on Grand Pre: A Book of Lyrics (1893)
Songs from Vagabondia (1894)
A Seamark: A Threnody for Robert Louis Stevenson (1895)
Behind the Arras: A Book of the Unseen (1895)
More Songs from Vagabondia (1896)
Ballads of Lost Haven: A Book of the Sea (1897)
By the Aurelian Wall: And Other Elegies (1898)
A Winter Holiday (1899)
Last Songs from Vagabondia (1901)
Ballads and Lyrics (1902)
Ode on the Coronation of King Edward (1902)
Pipes of Pan: From the Book of Myths (1902)

Pipes of Pan: From the Green Book of the Bards (1903)
Pipes of Pan: Songs of the Sea Children (1904)
Pipes of Pan: Songs from a Northern Garden (1904)
Pipes of Pan: From the Book of Valentines (1905)
Sappho: One Hundred Lyrics (1904)
Poems (1905)
The Rough Rider: And Other Poems (1909)
A Painter's Holiday, and Other Poems (1911)
Echoes from Vagabondia (1912)
April Airs: A Book of New England Lyrics (1916)
The Man of The Marne: And Other Poems (1918)
The Vengeance of Noel Brassard: A Tale of the Acadian Expulsion (1919)
Far Horizons (1925)
Later Poems (1926)
Sanctuary: Sunshine House Sonnets (1929)
Wild Garden (1929)
Bliss Carman's Poems (1931)

Drama
Bliss Carman & Mary Perry King. Daughters of Dawn: A Lyrical Pageant of a Series of Historical Scenes for Presentation with Music and Dancing (1913)
Bliss Carman & Mary Perry King. Earth Deities: And Other Rhythmic Masques (1914)

Prose Collections
The Kinship of Nature (1904)
The Poetry of Life (1905)
The Friendship of Art (1908)
The Making of Personality (1908)
Talks on Poetry and Life; Being a Series of Five Lectures Delivered Before the University of Toronto, December 1925 (Speech). transcribed by Blanche Hume. 1926.
Bliss Carman's Scrap-Book: A Table of Contents (Pierce, Lorne, editor) (1931)

Editor
The World's Best Poetry (10 volumes) (1904)
The Oxford Book of American Verse (U.S. editor) (1927)
Carman, Bliss; Pierce, Lorne, editors (1935). Our Canadian Literature: Representative Verse, English and French.

www.ingramcontent.com/pod-product-compliance
Lightning Source LLC
Chambersburg PA
CBHW060053050426
42448CB00011B/2428